VIOLIN
ONE HUNDRED
CLASSICAL
THEMES

Design by Hutton Staniford
Front cover photography by Stuart MacGregor

Order No. AM84153
Printed in the United Kingdom
by Caligraving Limited

ISBN: 978-0-7119-2587-9

For all works contained herein:
Unauthorized copying, arranging, adapting, recording, internet posting, public performance, or other distribution of the music in this publication is an infringement of copyright. Infringers are liable under the law.

Visit Hal Leonard Online at
www.halleonard.com

Contact us:
Hal Leonard
7777 West Bluemound Road
Milwaukee, WI 53213
Email: info@halleonard.com

In Europe, contact:
Hal Leonard Europe Limited
42 Wigmore Street
Marylebone, London, W1U 2RY
Email: info@halleonardeurope.com

In Australia, contact:
Hal Leonard Australia Pty. Ltd.
4 Lentara Court
Cheltenham, Victoria, 3192 Australia
Email: info@halleonard.com.au

A Musical Joke
(K.522, 4th movement) Mozart 4
A Policeman's Lot Is Not A Happy One
('The Pirates of Penzance') Sullivan 4
Air On The G String
(Suite No.3, 2nd movement) Bach 5
Autumn
(The Four Seasons, No.3, 1st movement) Vivaldi 6
Autumn
(The Four Seasons, No.3, 3rd movement) Vivaldi 6
Barcarolle
('The Tales of Hoffmann') Offenbach 7
Berceuse
(Dolly Suite Op.56) Fauré 8
Bolero
Ravel 8
Bridal March
('Lohengrin') Wagner 9
Brigg Fair
(An English Rhapsody) Delius 10
Brindisi
('La Traviata') Verdi 10
Che Farò Senza Euridice
('Orfeo ed Euridice') Gluck 11
Clarinet Concerto
(K.622, 2nd movement) Mozart 11
Clair de Lune
(Suite Bergamasque) Debussy 12
Eine Kleine Nachtmusik
(K.525, 1st movement) Mozart 12
Emperor Waltz
(Op.437) Strauss 13
España
(Rhapsody for Orchestra) Chabrier 14
Farandole
(L'Arlésienne Suite No.2) Bizet 14
For He Is An Englishman
('HMS Pinafore') Sullivan 15
Für Elise
Beethoven 15
Galop Infernal
('Orpheus in the Underworld') Offenbach 16
Gaudeamus Igitur
(Academic Festival Overture Op.80) Brahms 16
Gavotte
(Suite No.3, 3rd movement) Bach 17
Golliwogg's Cake Walk
(Children's Corner) Debussy 18
Gymnopédie No.1
Satie 18
Habanera
('Carmen') Bizet 19
He Shall Feed His Flock
('Messiah') Handel 20
Horn Concerto No.4
(K.495, 3rd movement) Mozart 20
Hornpipe
(The Water Music) Handel 21
Humoresque
(Op.101 No.7) Dvořák 21
Hungarian Dance No.5
Brahms 22
Jerusalem
Parry 22
Jupiter – I Vow To Thee, My Country
(The Planets Suite) Holst 23
La Calinda
('Koanga') Delius 24
Là Ci Darem La Mano
('Don Giovanni') Mozart 24
La Donna È Mobile
('Rigoletto') Verdi 25
Land of Hope and Glory
(Pomp & Circumstance March No.1 Op.39) Elgar 26
Largo – Ombra Mai Fù
('Xerxes') Handel 27
Les Sylphides
(Prelude Op.28 No.7) Chopin 27
March
(The Nutcracker Suite Op.71) Tchaikovsky 28
Minuet II
(Music For The Royal Fireworks) Handel 28
Morning
(Peer Gynt Suite No.1 Op.46) Grieg 29
Nimrod
(Enigma Variations Op.36) Elgar 30
Nocturne
('A Midsummer Night's Dream' Op.61) Mendelssohn 30
Non Più Andrai
('The Marriage of Figaro') Mozart 31
O For The Wings Of A Dove
('Hear My Prayer') Mendelssohn 32
Ode To Joy
(Symphony No.9 Op.125, 4th movement) Beethoven 33
One Fine Day
('Madame Butterfly') Puccini 33
Pavane
(Op.50) Fauré 34
Piano Concerto
(Op.16, 1st movement) Grieg 34
Piano Concerto – 'Elvira Madigan'
(K.467, 2nd movement) Mozart 35
Piano Concerto No.1
(Op.23, 1st movement) Tchaikovsky 35

Piano Concerto No.3
(Op.37, 1st movement) Beethoven 36
Piano Concerto No.5 – 'The Emperor'
(Op.73 2nd movement) Beethoven 36
Polovtsian Dances
('Prince Igor') Borodin 37
Pie Jesu
(Requiem Op.48) Fauré 38
Pomp & Circumstance March No.4
(Op.39) Elgar 38
Poor Wand'ring One
('The Pirates Of Penzance') Sullivan 39
Prelude
(L'Arlésienne Suite No.1) Bizet 40
Prelude to Act III
(Lohengrin) Wagner 40
Promenade
(Pictures At An Exhibition) Mussorgsky 41
Prince Igor Overture
Borodin 42
Radetzky March
(Op.228) Strauss 42
Romeo and Juliet
(Fantasy Overture) Tchaikovsky 43
Rondeau
('Abdelazar') Purcell 44
Rosamunde
(Entr'acte Act III) Schubert 44
Salut d'Amour
(Op.12) Elgar 45
Serenade
Schubert 45
Spartacus – 'The Onedin Line'
Khatchaturian 46
Spring
(The Four Seasons, No.1, 1st movement) Vivaldi 47
St Anthony Chorale
(Variations on a Theme of Haydn Op.56a) Brahms 47
Swan Lake
(Op.20, Opening of Act II) Tchaikovsky 48
Symphonie Fantastique
(Op.14, 4th movement) Berlioz 48
Symphony No.1
(Op.68, 4th movement) Brahms 49
Symphony No.3
(Op.90, 3rd movement) Brahms 49
Symphony No.3 – 'The Eroica'
(Op.55, 2nd movement) Beethoven 50
Symphony No.5
(Op.64, 2nd movement) Tchaikovsky 50
Symphony No.6 – 'The Pastoral'
(Op.68, 5th movement) Beethoven 51
Symphony No.6 – 'The Pathétique'
(Op.74, 1st movement) Tchaikovsky 51
Symphony No.9 – 'The Great'
(2nd movement) Schubert 52
Symphony No.9 – 'From the New World'
(Op.95, 2nd movement) Dvořák 52
Symphony No.9 – 'From the New World'
(Op.95, 4th movement) Dvořák 53
Symphony No.94 – 'The Surprise'
(2nd movement) Haydn 53
Take A Pair Of Sparkling Eyes
('The Gondoliers') Sullivan 54
Tannhäuser Overture
Wagner 54
The Blue Danube
(Waltz, Op.314) Strauss 55
The Merry Peasant
(Album for the Young Op.68 No.10) Schumann 56
The Trout Piano Quintet
(4th movement) Schubert 56
Toreador's Song
('Carmen') Bizet 57
Tristesse
(Étude Op.10 No.3) Chopin 57
Trumpet Voluntary
('The Prince of Denmark's March') Clarke 58
Valse
('Coppélia') Delibes 58
Violin Concerto
(Op.77, 2nd movement) Brahms 59
Violin Concerto
(Op.61, 2nd movement) Elgar 60
Violin Concerto
(Op.64, 2nd movement) Mendelssohn 60
Waltz
('The Sleeping Beauty' Op.66) Tchaikovsky 61
Wedding March
('A Midsummer Night's Dream' Op.61) Mendelssohn 62
William Tell Overture
Rossini 62
Your Tiny Hand Is Frozen
('La Bohème') Puccini 63
24th Caprice for Solo Violin
Paganini 64

A MUSICAL JOKE

(K.522, 4th movement) Mozart

A POLICEMAN'S LOT IS NOT A HAPPY ONE

('The Pirates of Penzance') Sullivan

AIR ON THE G STRING

(Suite No.3, 2nd movement) Bach

AUTUMN

(The Four Seasons, No.3, 1st movement) Vivaldi

AUTUMN

(The Four Seasons, No.3, 3rd movement) Vivaldi

BARCAROLLE

('The Tales Of Hoffmann') Offenbach

BERCEUSE

(Dolly Suite Op.56) Fauré

© Copyright 1991 Dorsey Brothers Limited, 8–9 Frith Street, London, W1V 5TZ.
All rights reserved. International Copyright secured.

Allegretto moderato

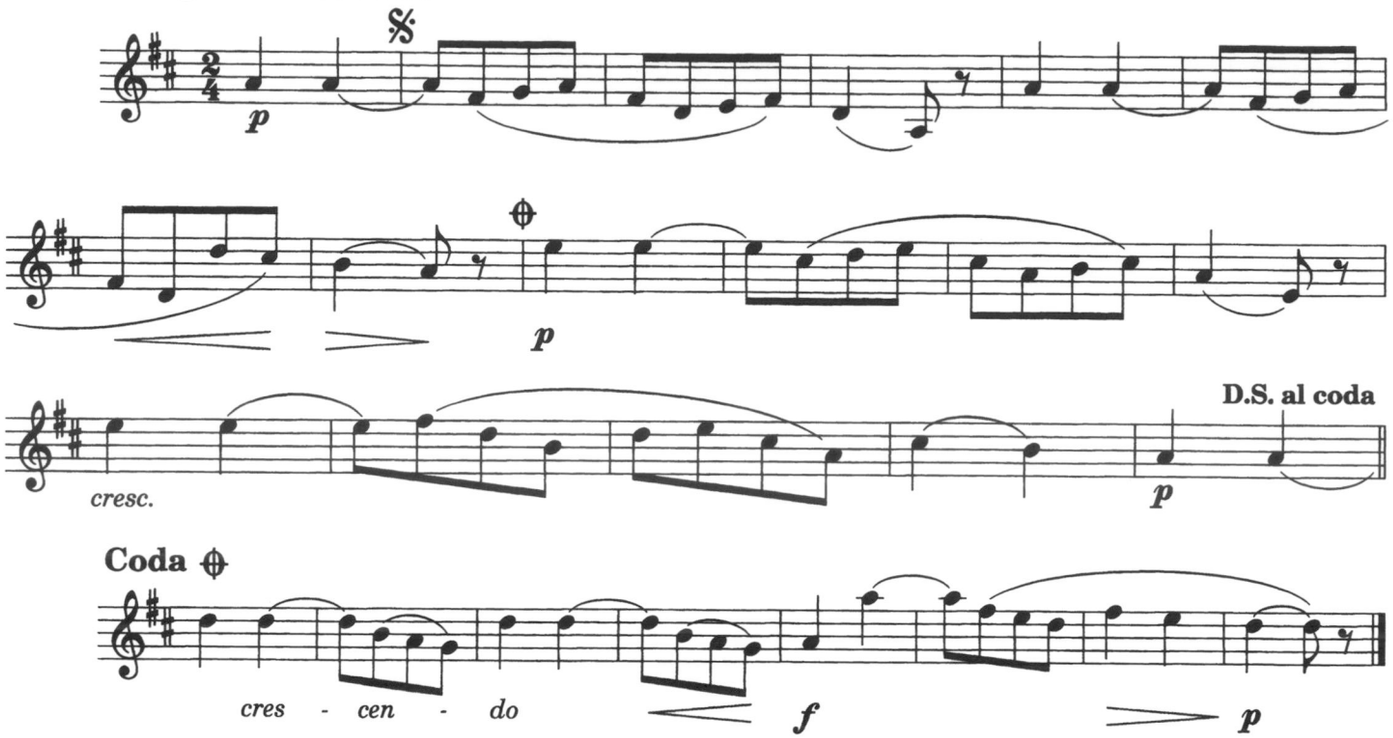

BOLERO

Ravel

© Copyright 1991 Dorsey Brothers Limited, 8–9 Frith Street, London, W1V 5TZ.
All rights reserved. International Copyright secured.

Tempo di Bolero moderato assai ♩=72

BRIDAL MARCH

('Lohengrin') Wagner

Moderato con moto

BRIGG FAIR

(An English Rhapsody) Delius

BRINDISI

('La Traviata') Verdi

CHE FARÒ SENZA EURIDICE

('Orfeo ed Euridice') Gluck

CLARINET CONCERTO

(K.622, 2nd movement) Mozart

CLAIRE DE LUNE

(Suite Bergamasque) Debussy

EINE KLEINE NACHTMUSIK

(K.525, 1st movement) Mozart

EMPEROR WALTZ

(op.437) Strauss

Tempo di valse

ben legato

ESPAÑA

(Rhapsody for Orchestra) Chabrier

Allegro con fuoco (♩.=80)

FARANDOLE

(L'Arlésienne Suite No.2) Bizet

Allegro vivo e deciso

FOR HE IS AN ENGLISHMAN

('HMS Pinafore') Sullivan

FÜR ELISE

Beethoven

GALOP INFERNAL

('Orpheus in the Underworld') Offenbach

GAUDEAMUS IGITUR

(Academic Festival Overture Op.80) Brahms

GAVOTTE

(Suite No.3, 3rd movement) Bach

[Allegro]

GOLLIWOGG'S CAKE WALK

(Children's Corner) Debussy

Allegro giusto

mf *sim.* *sff*

p *p* *f* *molto*

mf *sff*

ff

GYMNOPÉDIE NO.1

Satie

© Copyright 1991 Dorsey Brothers Limited, 8–9 Frith Street, London, W1V 5TZ.
All rights reserved. International Copyright secured.

Lent et doloureux

pp

p

HABAÑERA

('Carmen') Bizet

Allegretto quasi andantino

HE SHALL FEED HIS FLOCK

('The Messiah') Handel

Larghetto e piano

HORN CONCERTO NO.4

(K.495, 3rd movement) Mozart

Allegro vivace

HORNPIPE

(The Water Music) Handel

Alla Hornpipe

HUMORESQUE

(Op.101 No.7) Dvořák

Poco lento e grazioso

HUNGARIAN DANCE NO.5

Brahms

JERUSALEM

Parry

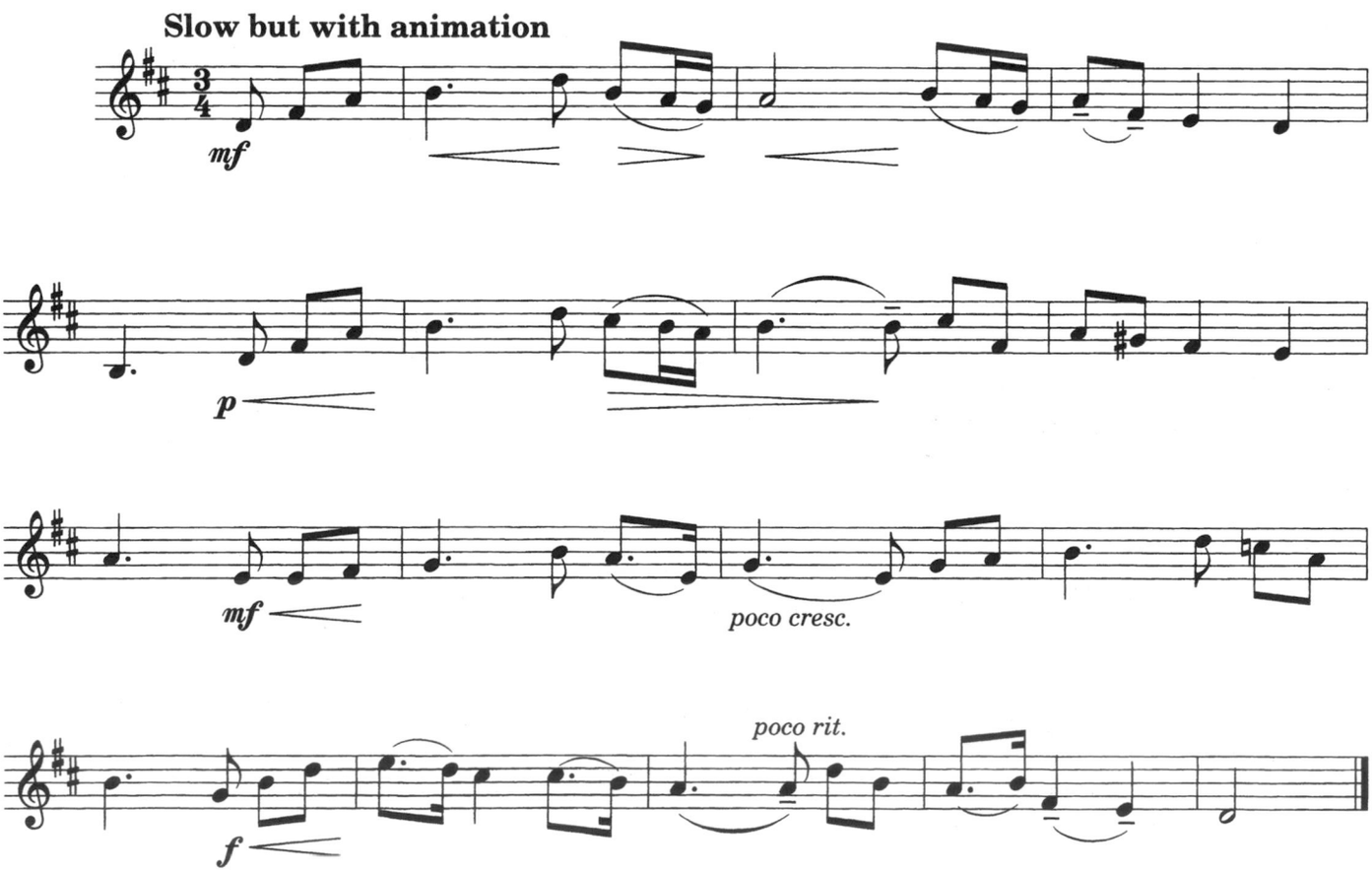

JUPITER - I VOW TO THEE, MY COUNTRY

(The Planets Suite) Holst

© Copyright 1991 Dorsey Brothers Limited, 8–9 Frith Street, London, W1V 5TZ
All rights reserved. International Copyright secured.

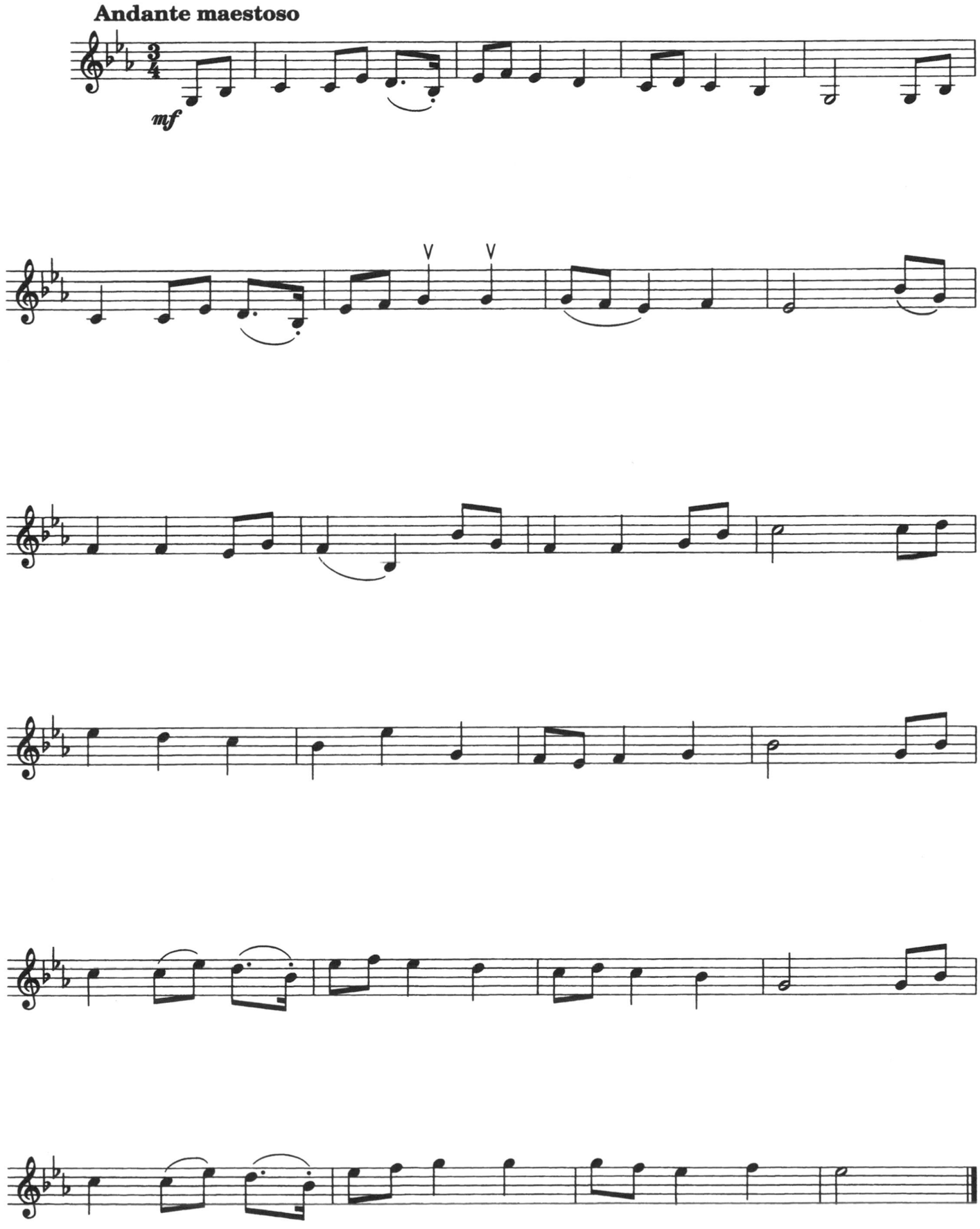

LA CALINDA

('Koanga') Delius

Moderato, con grazia

LÀ CI DAREM LA MANO

('Don Giovanni') Mozart

Andante

LA DONNA È MOBILE

('Rigoletto') Verdi

Allegretto

(*mf*) *con brio*

pp

leggiero

p

pp

con forza

LAND OF HOPE AND GLORY

(Pomp & Circumstance March No.1 Op.39) Elgar

LARGO - OMBRA MAI FÙ

('Xerxes') Handel

LES SYLPHIDES

(Prelude Op.28 No.7) Chopin

MARCH

(The Nutcracker Suite Op.71) Tchaikovsky

MINUET II

(Music for the Royal Fireworks) Handel

MORNING

(Peer Gynt Suite No.1 Op.46) Grieg

NIMROD

(Enigma Variations Op.36) Elgar

NOCTURNE

('A Midsummer Night's Dream' Op.61) Mendelssohn

NON PIÙ ANDRAI

('The Marriage of Figaro') Mozart

O FOR THE WINGS OF A DOVE

('Hear My Prayer') Mendelssohn

ODE TO JOY

(Symphony No.9 Op.125, 4th movement) Beethoven

ONE FINE DAY

('Madame Butterfly') Puccini

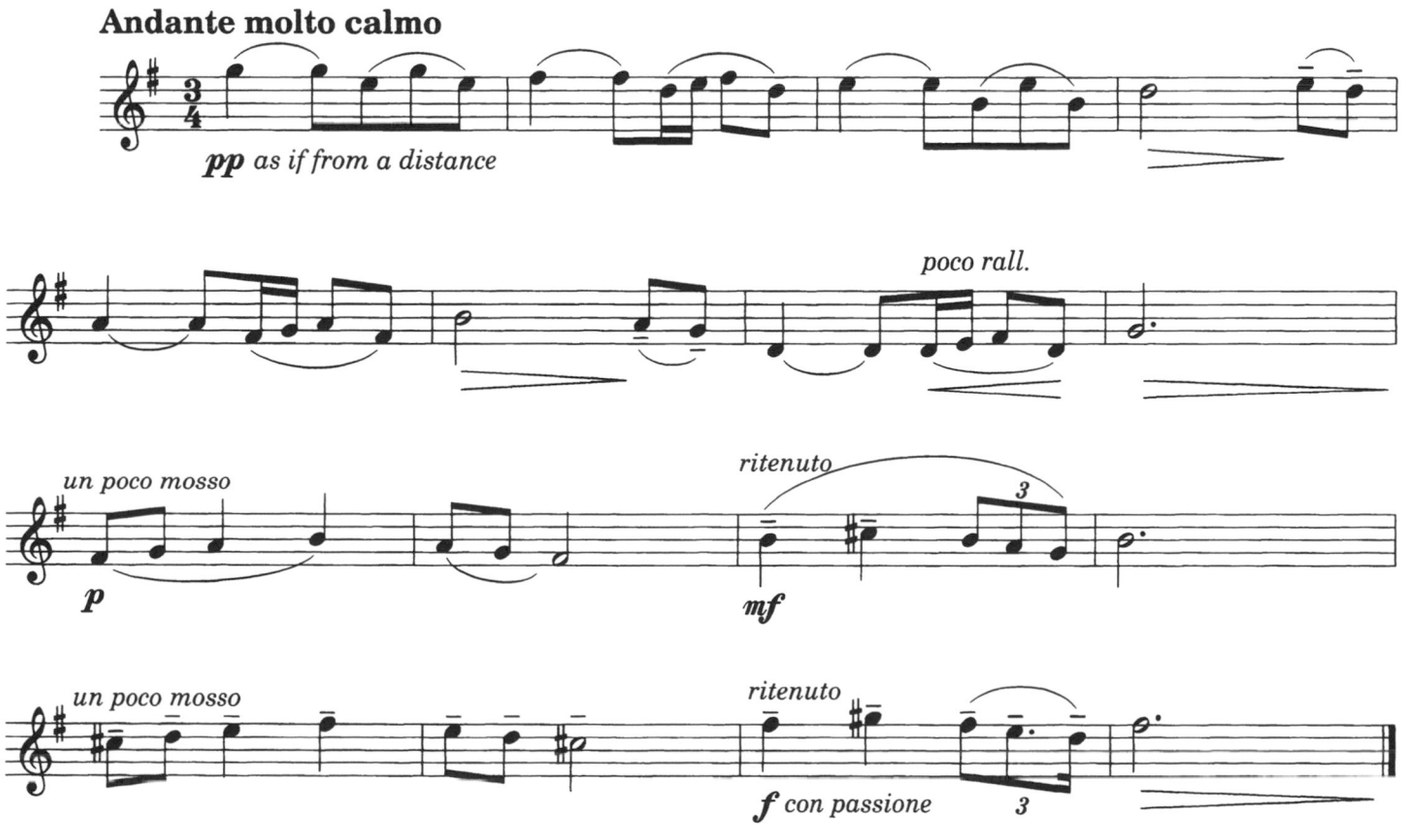

PAVANE

(Op.50) Fauré

© Copyright 1991 Dorsey Brothers Limited, 8–9 Frith Street, London, W1V 5TZ.
All rights reserved. International Copyright secured.

Allegro moderato

pp

pp

PIANO CONCERTO

(Op.16, 1st movement) Grieg

Allegro molto moderato ♩=84

p dolce

3

cresc. *f*

3

p

PIANO CONCERTO - 'ELVIRA MADIGAN'

(K.467, 2nd movement) Mozart

PIANO CONCERTO NO.1

(Op.23, 1st movement) Tchaikovsky

PIANO CONCERTO NO.3

(Op.37, 1st movement) Beethoven

Allegro con brio

PIANO CONCERTO NO.5 - 'THE EMPEROR'

(Op.73, 2nd movement) Beethoven

Adagio un poco mosso

POLOVTSIAN DANCES

('Prince Igor') Borodin

PIE JESU

(Requiem Op.48) Fauré

© Copyright 1991 Dorsey Brothers Limited, 8/9 Frith Street, London W1V 5TZ.
All rights reserved. International Copyright secured.

POMP & CIRCUMSTANCE MARCH NO.4

(Op.39) Elgar

POOR WAND'RING ONE

('The Pirates Of Penzance') Sullivan

Tempo di valse

PRELUDE

(L'Arlésienne Suite No.1) Bizet

Allegro deciso (tempo di marcia)

PRELUDE TO ACT III

('Lohengrin') Wagner

Molto vivace

PROMENADE

(Pictures At An Exhibition) Mussorgsky

Allegro giusto, nel modo russico; senza allegrezza, ma poco sostenuto

PRINCE IGOR OVERTURE

Borodin

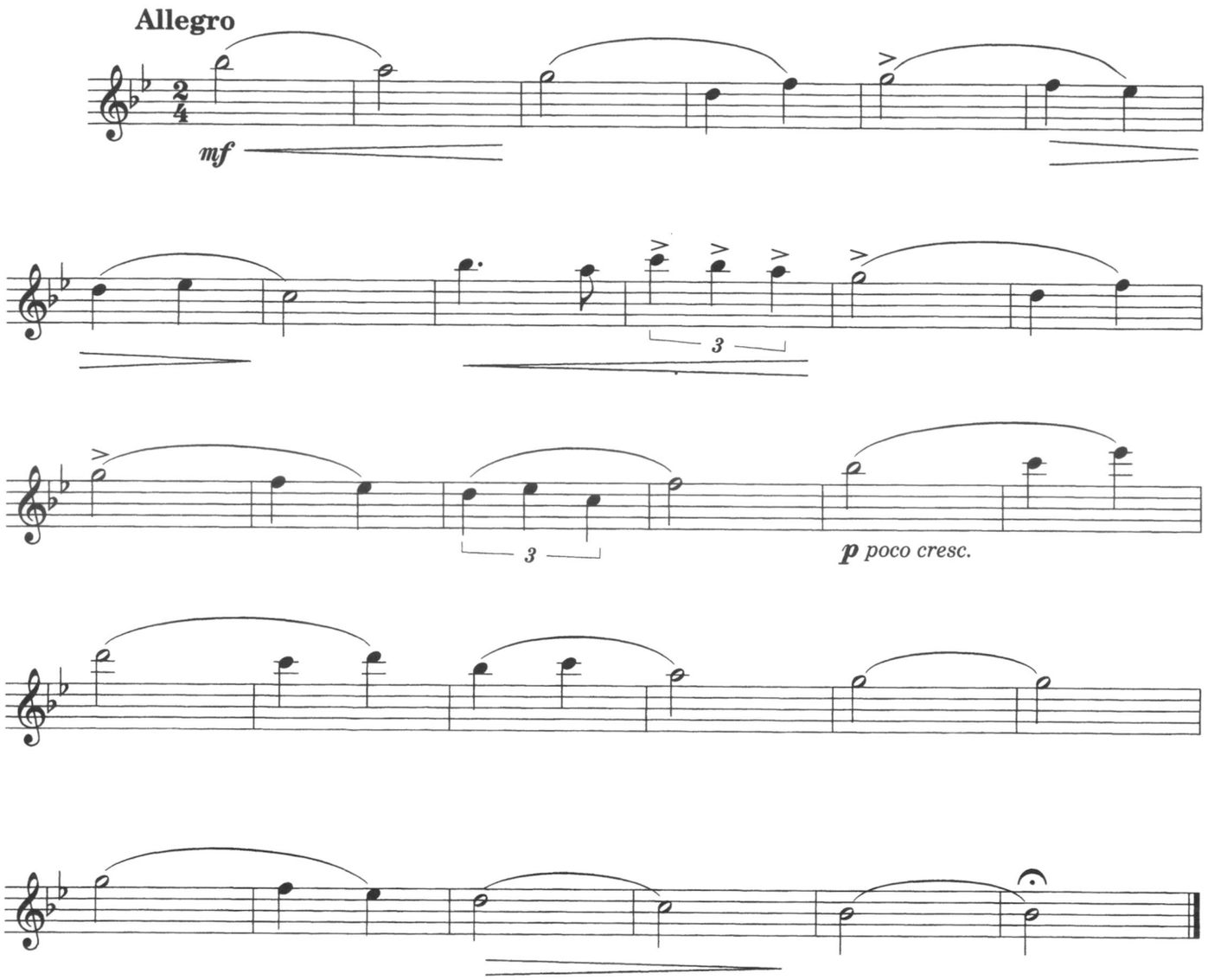

RADETSKY MARCH

(Op.228) Strauss

ROMEO AND JULIET

(Fantasy Overture) Tchaikovsky

Allegro giusto

(*mp*) *dolce*

cresc.

cresc.

mf cresc.

f

p dolce

RONDEAU

('Abdelazar') Purcell

ROSAMUNDE

(Entr'acte Act III) Schubert

SALUT D'AMOUR

(Op.12) Elgar

SERENADE

Schubert

SPARTACUS - 'THE ONEDIN LINE'

Khatchaturian

© Copyright 1991 Dorsey Brothers Limited, 8–9 Frith Street, London, W1V 5TZ.
All rights reserved. International Copyright secured.

SPRING

(The Four Seasons, No.1, 1st movement) Vivaldi

ST ANTHONY CHORALE

(Variations on a Theme of Haydn Op.56a) Brahms

SWAN LAKE

(Op.20, Opening of Act II) Tchaikovsky

SYMPHONIE FANTASTIQUE

(Op.14, 4th movement) Berlioz

SYMPHONY NO.1

(Op.68, 4th movement) Brahms

Allegro non troppo ma con brio

SYMPHONY NO.3

(Op.90, 3rd movement) Brahms

Poco allegretto

SYMPHONY NO.3 - 'THE EROICA'

(Op.55, 2nd movement)

Marcia funebre. Adagio assai. ♩=80

sotto voce

pp

sf

p

decresc.

p

SYMPHONY NO.5

(Op.64, 2nd movement) Tchaikovsky

Andante cantabile, con alcuna licenza ♩.=54

p dolce con molto espress.

animando

riten.

sostenuto

mf

p

animando

sostenuto

mf

p

SYMPHONY NO.6 - 'THE PASTORAL'

(Op.68, 5th movement) Beethoven

SYMPHONY NO.6 - 'THE PATHÉTIQUE'

(Op.74, 1st movement) Tchaikovsky

(teneramente, molto cantabile, con espressione)

SYMPHONY NO.9 - 'THE GREAT'

(2nd movement) Schubert

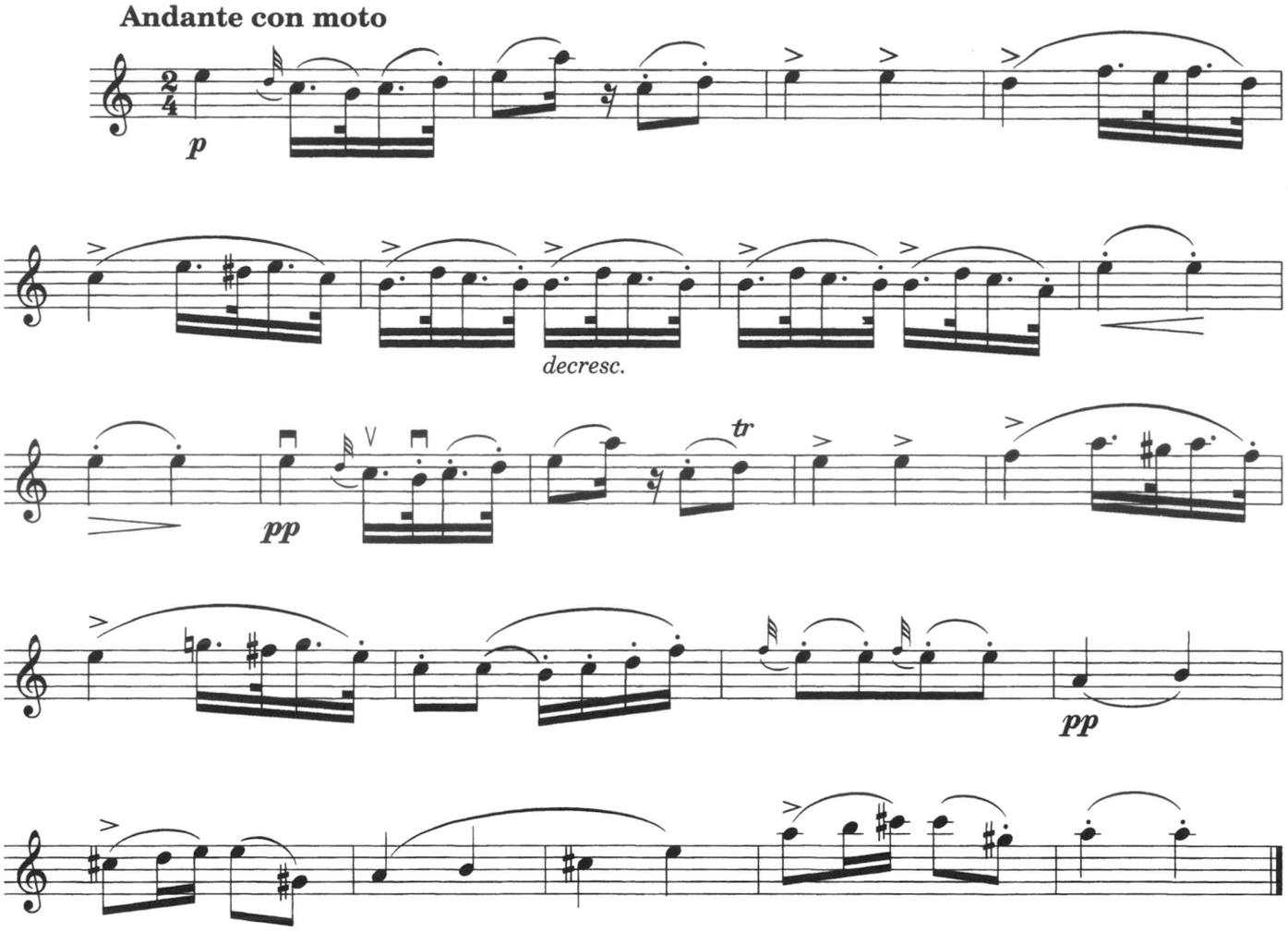

SYMPHONY NO.9 - 'NEW WORLD'

(Op.95, 2nd movement) Dvořák

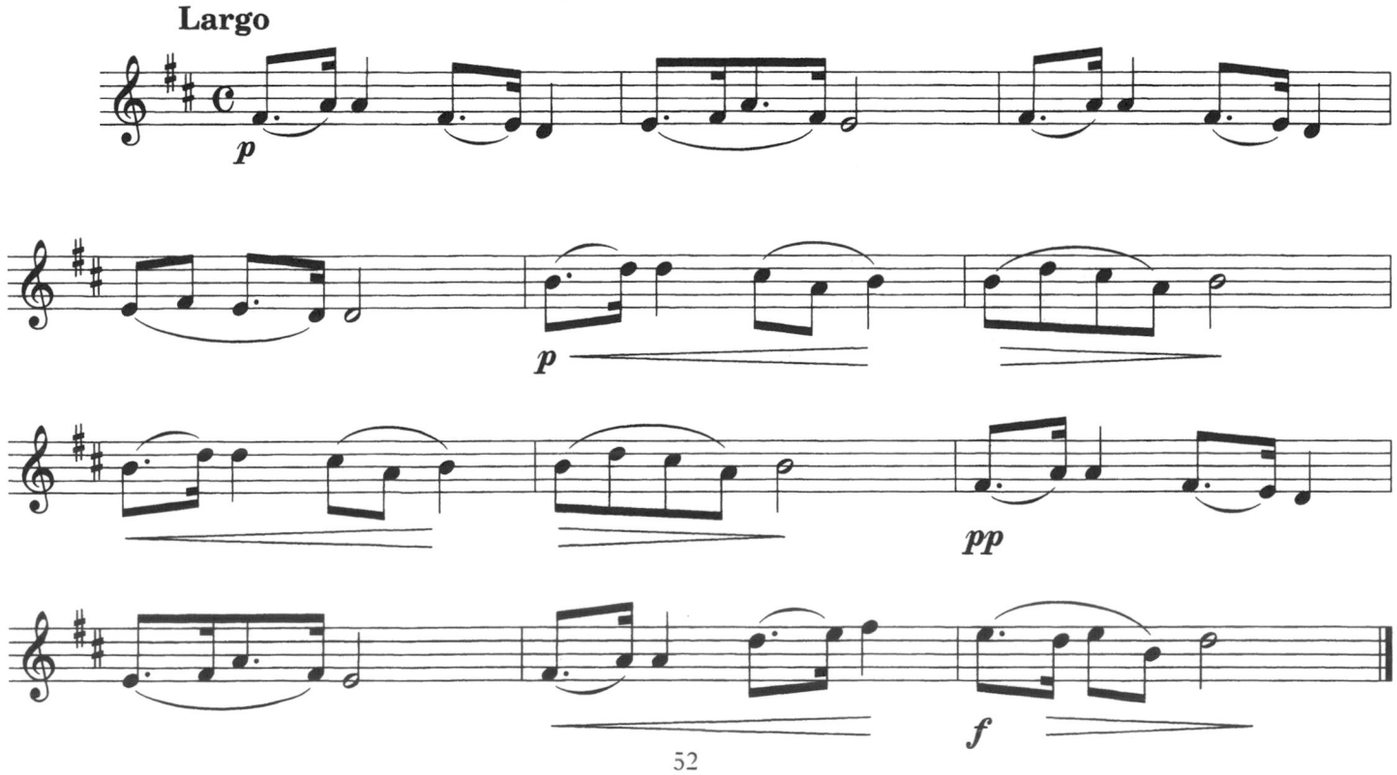

SYMPHONY NO.9 - 'NEW WORLD'

(Op.95, 4th movement) Dvořák

SYMPHONY No.94 - 'THE SURPRISE'

(2nd movement) Haydn

TAKE A PAIR OF SPARKLING EYES

('The Gondoliers') Sullivan

TANNHÄUSER OVERTURE

Wagner

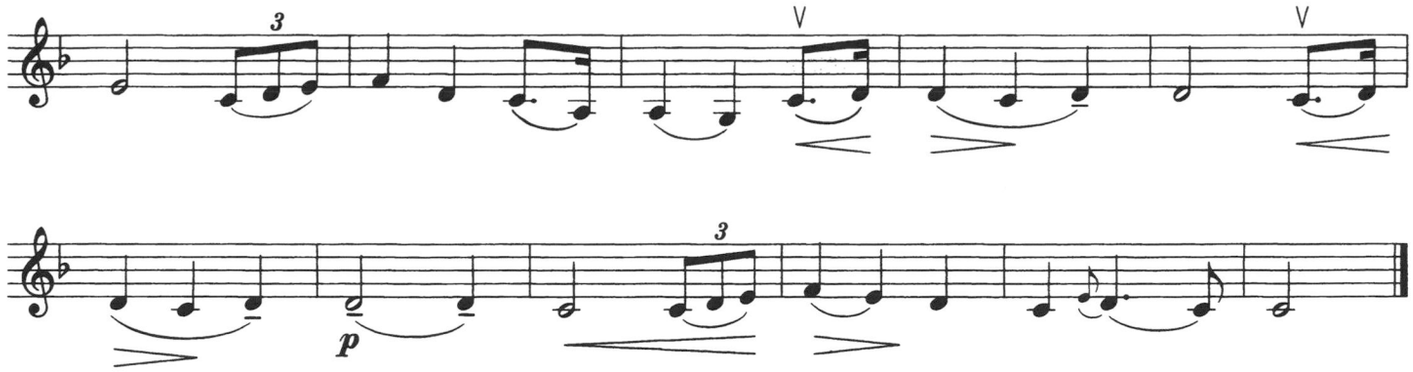

THE BLUE DANUBE

(Waltz, Op.314) Strauss

Tempo di valse

THE MERRY PEASANT

(Album for the Young Op.68 No.10) Schumann

THE TROUT PIANO QUINTET

(4th movement) Schubert

TOREADOR'S SONG

('Carmen') Bizet

Tristesse

(Étude Op.10 No.3) Chopin

TRUMPET VOLUNTARY

('The Prince of Denmark's March') Clarke

VALSE

('Coppélia') Delibes

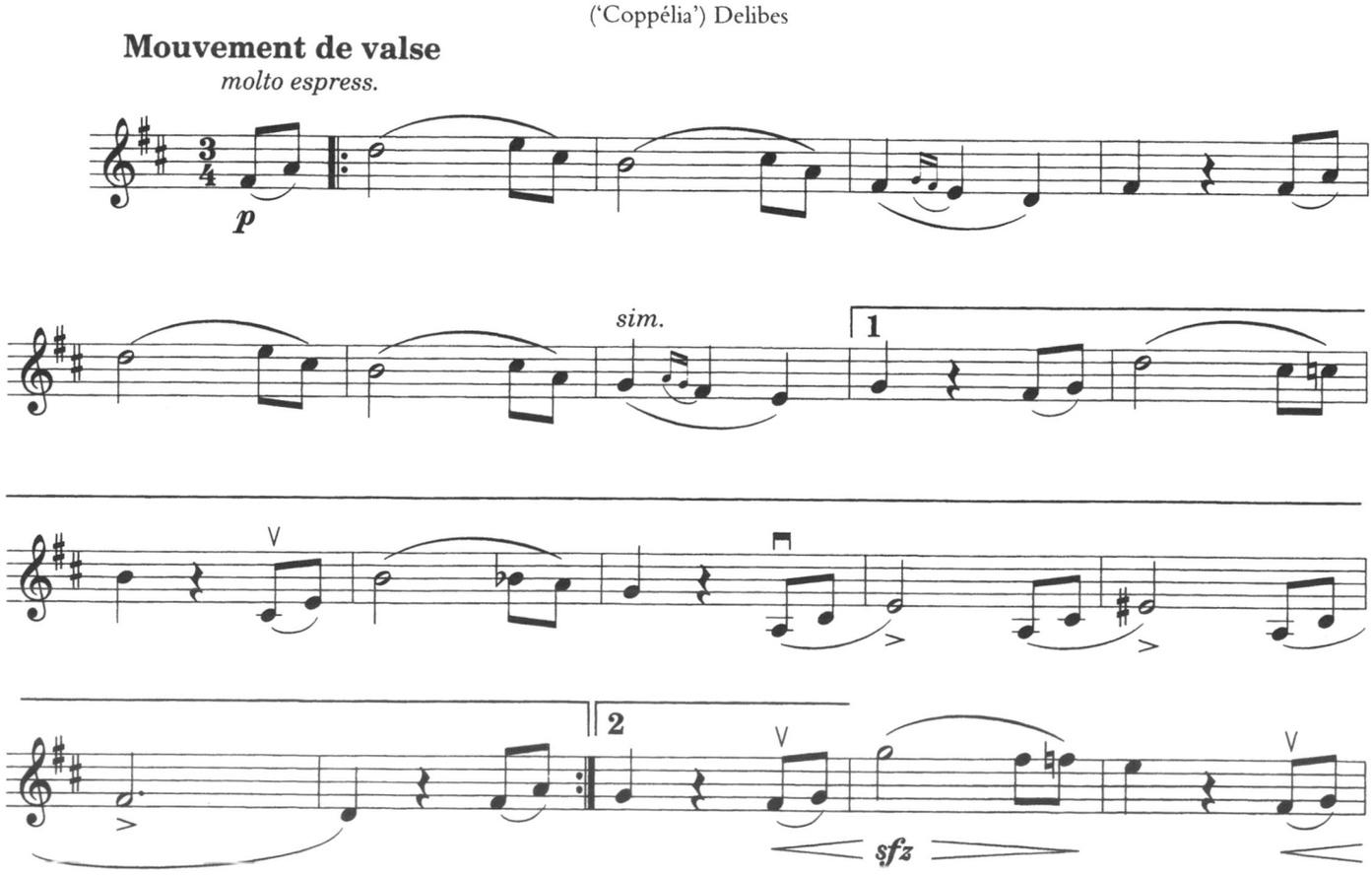

VIOLIN CONCERTO

(Op.77, 2nd movement) Brahms

Adagio

p dolce

p

dim.

p

8va

mf

loco

p

VIOLIN CONCERTO

(Op.61, 2nd movement) Elgar

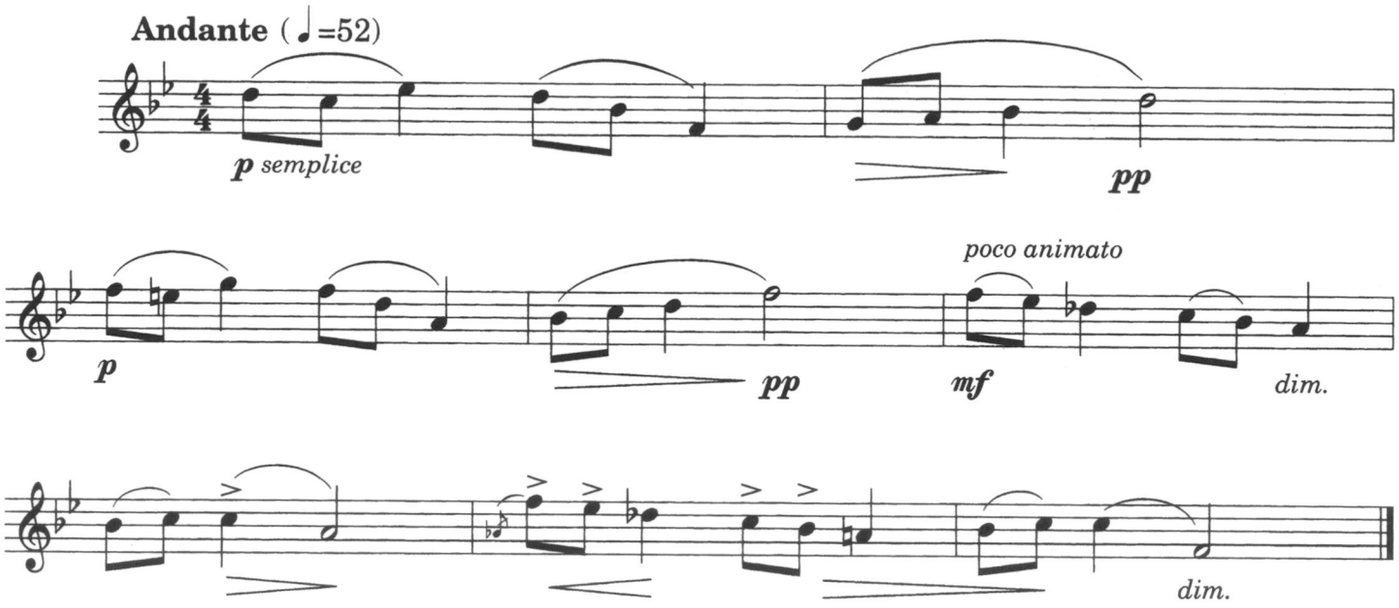

VIOLIN CONCERTO

(Op.64, 2nd movement) Mendelssohn

WALTZ

('The Sleeping Beauty' Op.66) Tchaikovsky

WEDDING MARCH

('A Midsummer Night's Dream' Op.61) Mendelssohn

WILLIAM TELL OVERTURE

Rossini

YOUR TINY HAND IS FROZEN

('La Bohème') Puccini

24TH CAPRICE FOR SOLO VIOLIN

Paganini